when I wear my leopard hat

for Ewan
best wishes + happy
birthday

when I wear my leopard hat

Dilys Rose

poems for young children by

Dilys Rose

illustrated by Gill Allan

SCOTTISH CHILDREN'S PRESS

for my Mum and Dad

First published in 1997 by
SCOTTISH CHILDREN'S PRESS
Unit 14, Leith Walk Business Centre,
130 Leith Walk, Edinburgh EH6 5DT
Tel: 0131 555 5950 • Fax: 0131 555 5018
e-mail: scp@sol.co.uk
http://www.taynet.co.uk/users/scp

Scottish Children's Press is an imprint of Scottish Cultural Press

British Library Cataloguing in Publication Data
A catalogue record for this book is available from the British Library

The publisher acknowledges subsidy from the
Scottish Arts Council towards the publication of this volume

THE SCOTTISH ARTS COUNCIL

ISBN: 1 899827 70 6

Printed and bound by Cromwell Press, Melksham, Wiltshire

Contents

Noises in the Night

Who's that running down the tenement stair?
Only Murdo's mammy with the ginger hair.

Who's that clumping up above my head?
Only Bobby Boddle, who should be in his bed.

What's that scratching on the window-pane?
Only Mr Teagle's cat, trying to get in.

What's that gushing like very heavy rain?
Only Jessie's bath water rushing down the drain.

What's that buzzing, will it ever stop?
Only Jock the watchman's old alarm clock.

What's that click and snuffle and bleep?
Only your imagination. Go to sleep!

I Love Sludge

I love sludge and I love slime,
I love grit and I love grime,
I love gunge and I love slush,
I love gloop and I love mush.

I love mess and I love muddles,
I love mud and I love puddles,
I love slip and I love slop,
I love plip and I love plop.

I love clatter and I love clutter,
I love flip and flop and flutter,
I love squelch and I love splash,
I love squish and splat and crash.

I love bump and I love bang,
I love clunk and clink and clang,
I love thud and I love thump,
I love bounce and bob and jump.

What's so great about being clean and quiet?

Sloth Song

I wish I were a sloth,
And lived life upside down,
The sky below, the ground above,
In the jungle instead of the town.

I wish I were a sloth,
Just a bundle of shaggy hair,
I'd never have to budge an inch,
'Cos nobody'd know I was there.

I wish I were a sloth,
So I could sleep all day,
Curled up in a cosy ball,
I'd dream my life away.

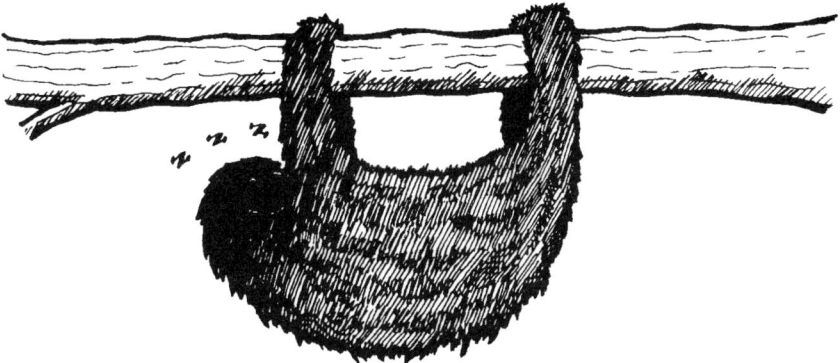

A Day at Portobelli

Kelly and Nellie
Had a day at Portobelli.
They played on the beach
Which was sandy but not shelly
(But smelly from the seaweed
And the stalls).
Nellie saw a fellae
Who had tattoos on his belly,
He was eating eels in jelly
From a jar.
Nellie lost Kelly
In the melée at the shows,
And Kelly lost a welly
On the waltzers.
They tried so many rides
That their eyes went wild and skelly
And both got home that night
Too tired to watch telly.

Ratty Toddler Rap

I'm dawdling down the road
With my head hung down.
I'm lingering and I'm loitering,
I'm wearing a frown.
I'm smearing slimy mud
From the ground on my knee,
I'm not answering to my name
'Cos my name's not me.
I'm stamping in puddles
And scowling at a log,
I'm sticking out my tongue
At a wee, yappy dog.
I'm not feeling good,
I'm not feeling nice,
My mum's so busy rushing
And she promised me an ice.
'Hurry up,' she's moaning,
So I run the wrong way.
I'm just not in the mood for this
I want to stop and play.

Baa Baa Beluga

Baa Baa Beluga,
Have you any blubber?
Aye, aye, cap'n,
Half a ton of it.
Some to keep me fit,
Some to keep me strong,
Some to keep me safe and warm
As I swim along.

So lay off!

Oodles of Noodles

Betty Spinetti eats loads of spaghetti,
She twirls it around in her bowl.
It wriggles like worms,
It squiggles and squirms,
So she sucks it and swallows it whole.

Dorothy Doodles eats oodles of noodles,
Just look at her shovel it in.
As Dorothy nibbles,
The sauce drips and dribbles
From her chin to her dress to her shin.

Anya Tatanya eats slabs of lasagne
Which ooze with melted cheese.
They slip and they slither,
They squish and they quiver
And slide down her throat with ease.

Mary Marconi eats more macaroni
Than anyone else I know.
She scoops up the loops
And gobbles the hoops
Saying: This is what makes me grow!

In Crail I Met a Snail

In Crail I met a snail,
In Capercleuch I lost a tooth,
In Milnathort I grew a wart,
In Forgandenny I found a penny,
In Lochnagar I saw a haar,
In Gretna Green I ate a bean,
In Lesmahagow mum made sago,
On Uplawmoor I made a tour,
In Penicuik I took a douk,
In Tobermory mum read a story,
In Bannockburn I was a girn,
In Scrabster I got a huge big blister,
In Machrihanish I tried to vanish.

Apollo and the Scaffy Wagon

Our street's very near
The centre of town
And all kinds of vehicles
Zoom up and down.
Fire engines, police cars,
Vans and ambulances,
Lorries, buses, motorbikes,
Milk carts and taxis.
I watch them from my window
Or close my eyes and guess
Which one makes the noise I hear
Becoming less and less.

My favourite of them all
Goes crank and cruck,
It stops and it starts
And it's full of muck.

Its head is back to front,
It's got teeth like a dragon
Can you guess what it is?
It's the scaffy wagon!

The driver is a tall, thin man,
Whose name is Apollo,
He chucks the rubbish in
And the dragon takes a swallow.
Apollo is a great grown-up,
He loves it when it snows,
He crunches up and down the street
And whistles as he goes.
He picks out all the pretty things
And laughs and sings and dances,
He decorates himself with junk,
Kicks up his heels and prances.
The best time's after Christmas
When folk throw out their trees,
He gathers up the tinsel
And wraps it round his knees.
He makes a cape from streamers
And a prickly crown from holly,
I just love Apollo
'Cos he's jolly, jolly, jolly.

Day-old Stubble

Hubble, bubble,
Froth and scrubble,
I watch dad soap
His day-old stubble.

He sloshes on foam
Then scrapes it clean
And rinses his cheeks
Of shaving cream.
He splashes his face
With ice-cold water,
Pats it dry
With a towel blotter.
Then – he says it's not scent
But he can't fool me –
He scooshes his chin
With a perfumed spray.
Now dad's ready
To face the day.

Hubble, bubble,
Froth and scrubble,
I'm glad dad's got rid
Of his scratchy old stubble.

Bumbaleerie Bumpkin

Bumbaleerie Bumpkin lives on the kitchen shelf,
At night when we are all asleep
He likes to go and help himself
To everything he finds to eat.

He nibbles at the biscuits,
He licks the strawberry jam,
He feasts on cheese and pickles
And finishes off the ham.

Bumbaleerie Bumpkin is our household elf,
At night when nobody can see
He likes to play a game of golf
With a stick of carrot and a pea.

His golf course is the kitchen floor
Where he plays till the sun comes up,
He hits the pea through a hole in the door,
Then goes back to sleep in an old teacup.

Brontosaurus Crunch

Barney Brontosaurus is a dancing buff,
He rocks and he rolls till he's out of puff,
He knocks down trees,
He mashes peas,
He makes a breeze
And he shimmies on his knees.

Brontosaurus Crunch,
Brontosaurus Crunch,
The whole world shakes
to the Brontosaurus Crunch.

Barney Brontosaurus is dancing mad,
He goes in the huff if a partner can't be had,
He sulks and moans,
He grumps and groans,
He rattles his bones,
And he kicks up stones.

Brontosaurus Crunch,
Brontosaurus Crunch,
The whole world shudders
to the Brontosaurus Crunch.

Betty Brontosaurus is a dancing ace,
She and Barney jive at a perfect pace,
They spin and skirl,
They twist and twirl,
They wiggle and they whirl,
They boogie and they birl.

Brontosaurus Crunch,
Brontosaurus Crunch,
The whole world jumps
to the Brontosaurus Crunch.

Mr Grumble and Mrs Grump

Mr Grumble and Mrs Grump
Lived in a hut by the city dump.
Mr Grumble was a chump,
Mrs Grump was a frump,
They ate their dinner off an old tree stump.

Mrs Grump and Mr Grumble
Were often heard to mump and mumble
That the roof of their hut was all a-crumble
And their home would surely tumble
On their heads with a thump.

Mr Grumble and Mrs Grump
Sucked up the jumble with an old foot pump.
Mr Grumble fumbled,
Mrs Grump bumbled,
As they fixed up their roof with a lump of junk.

Sphinx

Beside the Nile there stands the Sphinx,
She's made of stone, her hair's in kinks.
When the moon has rings she grins and winks
And it's a mystery what she thinks.

Sometimes she chases stars and sings
And flaps her decorated wings,
She doesn't care what tomorrow brings
Because tonight the moon has rings.

The Champion Sneezer

I know of a geezer
Called Ebeneezer,
They say he's the country's
Champion sneezer.
He trumpets like an elephant
At the zoo,
He can blow you down
With one ACHOO!
His handkerchief
Is as big as a sheet,
When he chases a sneeze
He sails down the street.

When I Wear My Leopard Hat

When I wear my leopard hat
I'm a fierce, enormous cat.
I creep along the kitchen floor
And then I spring and pounce and roar.
I growl like mad and show my claws,
I bare my teeth and AARGH! my jaws.
I'm going to pin you to the couch
And when I do, you'll squeal, 'Ouch, Ouch!
What is this wild beast doing to me,
When will it ever set me free?'

And then I'll purr and lick your nose,
I'll be myself and tickle your toes.

When I'm Bigger

When I'm bigger I will do
Everything you'd like me to,
I'll eat my food with a fork and spoon
And not shoot peas across the room.

I'll be polite, I'll wait my turn,
I won't grab a single cake or bun.
I'll always say PLEASE and THANK YOU VERY MUCH,
In shops I'll LOOK but I WON'T TOUCH.
I'll wear my hair neatly tied in place,
I'll wash my hands and even my face.
I'll share my games when friends come to play,
YOUR TURN NOW is what I'll say.

I won't bash my brother, I won't break toys,
I'll be more careful and I'll make less noise.
I won't play up when it's time for bed,
I'll kiss and cuddle and smile instead.

Yes, when I'm bigger I will do
Everything that you'd like me to,
But don't expect me to do them yet.
I'm STILL LITTLE. Please don't forget!

Me and My Shadow

When me and my shadow go out to play,
We stick together for company,
We touch at the toes by day and night
And never give each other a fright,
When I try to catch my shadow out,
It jumps back at me (but doesn't shout).

Sometimes my shadow skips ahead,
Sometimes it loiters behind,
Sometimes my shadow's ten foot long,
Sometimes it's hard to find
But it's always beside me wherever I go,
I'm never alone with my shadow.

My Mum's Tum

My mum's tum has blown up like a pumpkin
And I'm not allowed any bouncin' or jumpin'.
When I climb on her knee she says, 'Go Easy!'
She's worried I'll maybe squash the baby.
All mum wants to do these days is sit
And watch the telly, read or knit.
When the baby's born, her tum will surely shrink
Back to the shape it was before (I think).
And then mum will want to run and play
The way she used to do – Hip, hip, hooray!

But now mum only sighs when I dance about.
I wish that blinking baby would hurry and pop out.

I'm No Animal

When I run off with his door key,
Dad calls me a fly wee monkey.
When I hug him hard as I dare,
He calls me his grizzly bear.
When I dribble juice back into my cup,
He calls me a mucky pup.
When I pick holes in my beans on toast,
He calls me a messy beast.
When I say, 'I won't eat that!'
He calls me a spoiled brat.
When I say, 'Spoiled brat, spoiled brat!'
He calls me a copy cat.
But what I say is, it's not fair
To call me cat, or pup, or bear.
Surely even he can see,
I'm no animal, I'm just me.

The Garrulous Gargoyle

A garrulous gargoyle lives on the roof
Of the oldest building in town.
Some say he's stuck up, some say he's aloof,
I think he's just dizzy from looking down.
He's the one and only, he must be so lonely
With no one to talk to, up there on his own,
Unless an old pigeon stops off for a chat
About how he dive-bombed the Mulligan's cat
'Cos it crept up behind him and hissed and spat
And ruined his snooze on the Mulligan's mat.
Each time the poor gargoyle begins to speak,
The old pigeon pecks at his ear with his beak.
So the gargoyle is patient, he hears the bird out,
Then gives him a drink from his gurgling spout.

Nipper Zipper

On my purple pyjamas
Is a huge, big zipper,
It has a seal called Susie
Fixed on the clipper.
Suzy seal swims up and down
If I grip her by the flipper.
I've got to watch
She doesn't get caught
In the teeth of the zipper
Because they'd nip her.

Pollypoolipoppet

There was a boy called Ollie Crocket,
Who flew to the moon in a home-made rocket.
The rocket blew a socket
And Ollie couldn't stop it
From spinning round in circles
Like a chain and a locket,
Till Ollie said the magic word
POLLYPOOLIPOPPET!
The rocket shrunk till it was small
And Ollie put it in his pocket.
'That's much better now,' he said,
'As long as I don't drop it.
But if I'm to get home tonight
I think I'll have to walk it.'

Balloon

Blow me up and up and up,
With all the puff that you have left.
Pat me, pet me, pull me along.

Give me a face, a ribbon necklace,
Sing me a song.

Don't leave me alone
Till I shrivel and shrink
Or burst me,
'Cos then I'll be gone.

Zoe Didn't Go to the Zoo

Angus met an   **A**ardvark
Betty met a   **B**ison
Charmaine met a **C**ougar
     (and Polly met a python)

Deirdre met a   **D**romedary
Eddie met an   **E**lk
Franco met a   **F**lying Fish
     (and William met a whelk)

Gussie met a   **G**uppy
Hallie met a   **H**ake
Ina met an   **I**guana
     (and Sofia met a snake)

Jonathan met a **J**ackal
Krysia met a   **K**atydid
Lenny met a   **L**lama
     (and Cecil met a centipede)

Maxwell met a   **M**ongoose
Nicole met a   **N**ightingale
Oscar met an   **O**strich
     (and Wendy met a whale)

Pippa met a   **P**ipistrelle
Queenie met a   **Q**uail
Raul met a   **R**hino
Steven met a   **S**nail

Terry met a   **T**errapin
Ulla met an   **U**mbrella bird
Victor met a   **V**ampire bat
   (and Billy met a buzzard)

Winston met a   **W**ildebeest
Xanthe met an   o**X**
Yetta met a   mountain **Y**ak
      But poor
Zoe stayed home with **CHICKEN POX**.

Moody Trudy

When I'm in a mood
I won't do what I should,
You needn't bother coaxing me
There's no way I'll be good.

When I've got a fad
There's no way I'll be had,
If I want chips then I want chips,
If mum says no, I'll ask my dad.

When I'm being silly
I'm like that willy-nilly,
There's no use talking sense to me,
My head's a piccalilli.

Mum's Night Out

My mum's put some shoes on
She hardly ever wears,
She's done her hair up funny
And hung spangles from her ears.

She smells of soap and gardens
And jangles when she walks,
She rushes round the bedroom
Trying on all her frocks.

When she puts her handbag by the door,
Beside her favourite coat,
And doesn't bother me at all,
I know she's going out.

She races round the kitchen
Putting things away,
'Tess will be here soon,' she says,
'Then you and she can play.

Please try not to be a pest,
Or Tess won't come again,
And remember to go straight to bed
As soon as Tess says when.'

I don't say yes, I don't say no,
But then I hear a knock,
I jump and yell and clap my hands,
Mum quickly checks the clock.

A kiss from mum then off she goes,
Clicking down the street,
She doesn't like to hang about
And see me start to greet.

But when mum's gone the fun begins,
My tears were just pretend,
Tess knows so many brilliant tricks
That I don't want the night to end.

We scoff the snacks mum left us
On a fancy patterned plate.
Tess doesn't seem to mind a bit
If I run wild and stay up late.

She grips me by the ankles
And twirls me like a top,
And then we do some somersaults,
And then I learn to hop.

I get a bit dizzy and my head feels fizzy
And the walls go spinning round,
The light bulb swings and I bump into things
And I can't keep my feet on the ground.

Then Tess starts a story
About a magic spotted snake.
I didn't hear the end of it –
I couldn't stay awake.

Selected titles also available from
SCOTTISH CHILDREN'S PRESS

An A–Z of Scots Words for young readers
1 899827 03 X

Aiken Drum: a story in Scots for young readers
Anne Forsyth; illustrated by Dianne Sutherland; 1 899827 00 5

Bobby Boat and the Big Catch: an Aberdeen Adventure
Thomas Chalmers; illustrated by Billy Dobbie; 1 899827 54 4

Bobby Boat in Trouble at Sea: an Oban Adventure
Thomas Chalmers; illustrated by Billy Dobbie; 1 899827 55 2

Classic Children's Games from Scotland
Kendric Ross; illustrated by John MacKay; 1 899827 12 9

Kitty Bairdie: a story in Scots for young readers
Anne Forsyth; illustrated by Dianne Sutherland; 1 899827 01 3

Sandy MacStovie's Monster
Moira Miller; illustrated by Rob Dee; 1 899827 27 7

Teach the Bairns to Bake: Traditional Scottish Baking for Beginners
Liz Ashworth; 1 899827 24 2

Teach the Bairns to Cook: Traditional Scottish Recipes for Beginners
Liz Ashworth; 1 899827 23 4

Wallace, Bruce, and the War of Independence
Antony Kamm; illustrated by Jennifer Campbell; 1 899827 15 3

Wee Willie Winkie and other rhymes for Scots children
Fiona Petersen (ed.); 1 899827 17 X

The Wild Haggis an the Greetin-faced Nyaff
Stuart McHardy; illustrated by Alistair Phimister; 1 899827 04 8

for further information on these or any of our other titles,
please contact **SCOTTISH CHILDREN'S PRESS**, Unit 14,
Leith Walk Business Centre, 130 Leith Walk, Edinburgh EH6 5DT